Diane Guilford

gen-X
Y-faith?

GETTING REAL WITH GOD

*May you be richly blessed
in your new parish.
Charlie and Kay*

Ross Lockhart

gen-X Y-faith?

GETTING REAL WITH GOD

Northstone

Editors: James Taylor and Michael Schwartzentruber
Cover/interior design: Margaret Kyle
Cover art: Copyright © Charity A. Breiner,
www.perplexity.cjb.net. Used with permission.
Proofreading: Dianne Greenslade
Credits:

A New Creed from *Voices United: The Hymn and Worship Book of the United Church of Canada*. The United Church Publishing House, 1996, p. 918. Used with permission.

A paraphrase of Ephesians 3:20-21 from *The Book of Alternative Services of the Anglican Church of Canada,* copyright 1985 by the General Synod of the Anglican Church of Canada. Used with permission.

"Come and Find the Quiet Centre" by Shirley Erena Murray, copyright 1992 Hope Publishing Co., Carol Stream, IL 60188. All rights reserved. Used by permission.

Scripture taken from *The Message*, copyright by Eugene H. Peterson, 1993, 1994, 1995. Used by permission of NavPress Publishing Group.

Scripture from the *New Revised Standard Version* of the Bible, copyright 1989 by the Division of Christian Education of the National Council of Churches of Christ in the United States of America. Used by permission.

Two prayers from *The Edge of Glory: Prayers in the Celtic Tradition* by David Adam, (original publisher, Harrisburg, PA: Morehouse Publishing, 1985) used by permission of SPCK, England. All rights reserved.

"The House of Our God" by Jim Manley in *All God's Children Sing* (Kelowna: Wood Lake Books, 1992) #72. Used by permission.

Northstone Publishing acknowledges the financial support of the Government of Canada through the Book Publishing Industry Development Program for its publishing activities.

NORTHSTONE PUBLISHING is an imprint of **WOOD LAKE BOOKS INC.,** an employee-owned company, and is committed to caring for the environment and all creation. Northstone recycles and reuses and encourages readers to do the same. Resources are printed on recycled paper and more environmentally friendly groundwood papers (newsprint), whenever possible. The trees used are replaced through donations to the Scoutrees For Canada Program. A portion of all profit is donated to charitable organizations.

National Library of Canada
Cataloguing in Publication Data
Lockhart, Ross, 1977-
Gen-X Y-faith?: getting real with God/
Ross Lockhart.
ISBN 1-896836-58-5
1. Youth – Religious life. 2. Spiritual life
    – Christianity. I. Title.
BV4531.3.L62 2003   248.8'3   C2003-910944-5

Published by Northstone Publishing,
an imprint of Wood Lake Books Inc.
Kelowna, British Columbia, Canada
www.joinhands.com

Printed in Canada at Transcontinental Printing

Dedication

In memory of my Father,
George Ernest Lockhart

"Come to me, all you who are weary and burdened,
and I will give you rest."
Matthew 11:28

Contents

Acknowledgments

There are a great number of folks responsible for shaping my "practical divinity" over the years and helping me move through my own faith development of resistance, rediscovery and relationship with God.

In particular, I wish to acknowledge the sisters and brothers in Christ in the various Christian communities that I have called home over the years.

Rev. Dr. Allan Saunders and Sturgeon Creek United Church in Winnipeg, Manitoba whose rich and faithful soil proved fertile growing space for God's grace in my life.

Rev. Dr. David McKane and Royal York Road United in Etobicoke, Ontario who helped shape my identity as a youth pastor and who greatly valued ministry to youth and young adults.

Rev. Dr. Susan MacAlpine-Gillis and Cole Harbour-Woodside United Church in Dartmouth, Nova Scotia, who gave me enthusiastic support in my role as associate pastor and unfailingly attempted to add a few pounds through good old-fashioned Maritime cooking.

Friends and colleagues in theological education at Emmanuel College in The University of Toronto for their support and challenge along the way. A special thank you to Professor Phyllis Airhart, for reading this work in its infancy and providing some much needed critical feedback before I got too far off track.

I am indebted also to the good folks at Wood Lake Books who shared my passion and vision for connecting Generation X with the good news of Jesus. In particular, I wish to thank Lois Huey Heck and Jim Taylor for their editorial skill and wisdom in bringing this project to fruition.

Finally, a thank you to my family. To Maisie, my adorable and abiding Airedale terrier, who faithfully defended the computer throughout this project as well as offering editorial comments while napping in her chair. And above all, my greatest appreciation to my wife Laura whose own call to ministry and passion for God helped reveal to me Christ's promise of an abundant life. May our future be blessed with the joy that discipleship brings and grounded in the hope of John Wesley's closing witness, "Best of all, God is with us."

A Gen Xer
goes to church

One generation shall laud your works to another,
and shall declare your mighty acts.
Psalm 145:4

The old preacher stumbled towards the pulpit with a solemn, tired face. His robes, bursting at the seams, suggested a few too many teacup and cookie visits with the local senior citizens. Putting on his dusty trifocals, the aging vicar surveyed his flock. Under his gaze the congregation shifted their weight uneasily, betraying their unfocused minds and heavy hearts. The sanctuary was about as lively as a room full of carbon monoxide.

Sneaking in late, I sat in the last pew and looked around to discover that yet again I was the only person under 50 years old in the church. This day, as every other Sunday, I desperately hoped and prayed for something in the sermon that might speak God's Word in a way that made sense and connected with my own Generation X culture.

Unfortunately, what flowed from the tired lips of the preacher had nothing to do with a sense of belonging, the quest for spirituality, the great moral dilemmas of our age, or who Jesus is for us today. Instead, the preacher, seemingly itching for retirement (that state having been long ago achieved by his congregation), rambled through a mind-numbing sermon that could have put Richard Simmons to sleep. Did the preacher really think that recycled images and stories from World War II, lyrics from 1960s protest songs, and a liberal sprinkling of politically correct language made his sermon cutting edge? And of course, his references to "the good old days" when the church was full of young people only caused increased depression in the aging congregation as they looked around and saw their community less as a living church and more as a waiting room for heaven. If anyone's soul was in need of nourishment that day it would have shriveled right down to its roots even before the benediction was pronounced.

As I staggered out of the building at the end of the service, I was reminded once again of the serious trouble the mainline churches are in. Going to a church like this one is about as much fun as a visit to your local proctologist!

Introduction

But I still haven't found what I'm looking for…
U2

Gen Xers have been described by author Douglas Coupland as the first generation raised without religion.[1] And in many ways this is true. Mainline churches across North America are facing a crisis because the majority of people in them fall into the "blue rinse crowd" of our grandparents. Genuine attempts by the mainline Christian churches to attract younger members have often

[1] Douglas Coupland, *Life after God* (New York: Pocket Books, 1994).

produced poor results, perhaps because the leadership has felt the need to water down the religious message in order to make it more appealing to baby boomers. The result, according to experts, is that most Xers (roughly defined as those born between 1965-1980) see this watering down by baby boomers and others as a public confession that they're ashamed of their beliefs.[2]

As a result, a large number of Gen Xers have had little more than a simplistic "connect-the-dot Jesus" Sunday school exposure to God, or an equally meaningless one as young adults. Instead of receiving inspiration to fire up their lives, Gen Xers are left with the impression that the Christian church is at best an ecclesiastical Titanic that is helplessly slipping into the deep, dark, and icy seas of history.

Yet we remain a thirsty generation. If indeed we are the first generation raised without religion then we surprisingly continue

[2] For more on Gen X versus the baby boomers, see Lauren Winner's article "A return to tradition? Gen X revisited" in *Christian Century* (November 8, 2000). Note her argument on page 1147 that "Xers' skin crawls when they meet boomers who water down the gospel and reduce it merely to a social justice message rather than integrating that message with the proclamation of Jesus Christ."

to show an ongoing interest in matters of spirituality. Most Xers will give more than a passing glance to books on new age or Eastern religions when pausing in the Spirituality section of the local bookstore to scan the titles. It is as if one of the marketing tools of our generation, "Obey Your Thirst," has carried over to a deep longing for a connection with the Divine.

In fact, humankind's longing for more than this world has to offer is nothing new at all. Take the ancient song of King David found in the book of Psalms:

> *As the deer pants for the water, so my soul longs after you;*
> *You alone are my heart's desire and I long to worship you.*[3]

Or as an early Christian bishop named Augustine once confessed to God, "You have made us for yourself, and our heart is restless until it rests in you."[4]

[3] Psalm 42, verse 1 as printed in *Voices United* (Toronto: United Church Publishing House, 1996) p. 766.

[4] Saint Augustine, *Confessions* (Oxford: Oxford University Press, 1991) p. 4.

Yet for all this desire to find meaning and purpose for our lives, most Xers remain resistant to God, and many for very good reasons indeed. Sometimes it feels like organized religion can throw up as many roadblocks in rediscovering God as a police department trying to stop O.J. Simpson fleeing from justice!

As a student minister, I knew that most of my friends did not go to church but still thought of me as a fairly normal and average kind of guy. Many of them began asking me simple questions about the Christian faith with a gentle curiosity, trusting that I was not going to hit them over the head with a Bible or anything like that! I discovered, however, that there were very few resources available to help answer their sincere questions. So I responded by crafting this work – an introduction to Christian Spirituality from someone who speaks and thinks from a Gen X perspective.

I hope the result is a fairly safe and sophisticated way to help Xers connect their deepest thirst for spirituality with the deepest longing of God for relationship with each and every one of us. This book is based on a threefold sequence that I have found true in my own Gen X experience of God and I hope it might speak a word of truth to others. Perhaps there are many out there who can connect with these three stages of resisting the Divine, longing to rediscover the Holy in their midst, and finally being willing to take tentative steps towards a relationship with God.

Although this book was mainly written for those who grew up watching Captain Stubing and friends on *The Love Boat* while we wore our Bo & Luke or Daisy Duke p.j.'s, and ate our Count Chocula cereal out of a He-man or Jem and the Holograms bowl, I have written it also for those who have a great love for Gen Xers and long for them to explore issues of faith. Although there will always be generational differences (one group's favorite comedy might be *I Love Lucy*, another's might be *Seinfeld*) there must be a way that we can speak authentically to each generation and share our stories of faith and spirituality.

For example, as we Gen Xers mature and grow, we are starting to share some deep questions with previous generations:

- A dead-end job may lead us to question, "What am I really meant to do with my life?"

- Happening upon the scene of a terrible car accident may prompt us to ask, "Is there any order in the universe?"
- The sickness of a friend may cause us to struggle with "What sources of strength can I fall back on during times of trouble?"
- The birth of one's first child can lead to questions like "How do I properly give thanks for this miracle of new life?" or "What values and moral foundations am I going to raise this little person on?"
- The death of a family member may lead us to questions such as, "Why are we here at all and what happens after death?" "Is there a unifying purpose for life or are we just existing by pure luck?" "What is the driving source of my dreams and desires?"

Even though Generation X may be the first generation raised without religion, we still need to believe in something that will engage the complexities and ambiguities of life, not avoid them. As a skeptical generation we are wary of but not opposed to searching for "the truth."

The faded exterior of the building beside my theological college at the University of Toronto bears in giant letters above the door way this message:

THE TRUTH WILL MAKE YOU FREE

As I sit outside my college eating lunch, I watch people read the message as they go by. Often they will turn to a friend and say out of curiosity, "What does that mean?" Very few know that it is the words of Jesus spoken to his disciples to describe the journey of faith humans are on.

Jesus said, "If you hold to my teaching, you are really my disciples. Then you will know the truth, and the truth will set you free." [5]

From sitting and watching this daily spectacle, it is clear that often the Christian message is lost from one generation to another. Every generation needs to reinterpret this message, to wrestle and

[5] John 8:31, *New International Version* (Grand Rapids, Michigan: Zondervan, 1978).

struggle with it, in order to be awakened to the truth that sets us free.

Read then a bit with me and determine what's true for your own life and what's out there that might just open your heart, mind, and soul to a new kind of freedom.

1

Resisting God

Come, O thou Traveller unknown,
whom still I hold, but cannot see! [1]

Jacob the Gen Xer

Jacob was quite a guy. Even though he lived a long time ago – with his story recorded in the first book of the Bible – I think he'd fit in very nicely with today's Gen X crowd. You see, Jacob was a

---

[1] Charles Wesley, "Jacob Wrestling the Angel," *Methodist Hymn Book* (Toronto: Methodist Publishing House, 1884) p. 265.

scrapper from day one. Jacob grew up like most kids, fighting often with his brother and trying to win the favor of his parents. He played hard, was shrewd in business, and even pulled dirty tricks on his friends and relatives in order to gain wealth and power. He was in every way a self-made man. No doubt, he would have turned heads in the neighborhood when he returned home for Sunday dinner in a shiny new BMW.

When it came to religion, Jacob felt no need of God even though he came from a very religious family. Jacob's grandparents Abraham and Sarah and his parents Isaac and Rebekah were all devout folks who practiced their religion seriously. But it didn't seem to rub off on Jacob. God wasn't even on Jacob's radar screen.

Instead, Jacob was focused on what he could get out of life for himself. He didn't spend much time thinking about what existed beyond his desire for wealth and personal happiness. As far as Jacob was concerned, if God even existed, God was more of an absentee landlord, someone who put things in motion by creating the universe and then abandoned the scene refusing to return even to fix a leaky toilet. Jacob would probably agree with Bette

Midler's extremely cheesy 1980s pop hit entitled *God is watching us from a distance*. His family could keep their faith; he would keep his own distance.

The Head of Helga

If Jacob were alive today, his skepticism and personal drive would help him fit in nicely with most Gen X crowds in North America. After all, we too are for the most part a skeptical generation – and often with good reason.

I learned one of these lessons long ago when my friends and I encountered the Head of Helga.

The Red River Exhibition marked two important events for teenagers growing up in my hometown – the end of school and the beginning of summer. Weeks in advance my friends and I would buy "all you can ride" day passes from a local convenience store and make a pact to stay until we had tried every ride at the fair at least twice! Unfortunately, when we got to the Exhibition, everyone else had the same idea. Our excitement soon evaporated in the sweltering heat and long queues. And so, on one occasion, after standing in an insane line-up for a couple of rides, we decided to change our strategy. In a brief huddle, we decided to spend the rest of the day seeking out the cheesiest rides and attractions we could find – which of course also had the added bonus of the shortest line-ups at the fair.

As we made our way to the edge of the fairgrounds we discovered in an obscure and deserted area a display entitled "THE HEAD OF HELGA." The front of the tent depicted a very beautiful woman's face, apparently lacking a corresponding torso. Her image was projected on a colorful blood red background. Of course, being teenage boys, this attraction combined our only two real interests – women and horror movies. As we approached this tabernacle of mystery, a cheesy tape-recorded "disembodied" voice proclaimed at steady 30-second intervals,

Is it the head of John the Baptist? Is it the head of Marie Antoinette? Noooooo! It's the HEAD OF HELGA!

Needless to say we were more than a little curious. So we entered into the sanctuary of Helga seeking a greater understanding of this awe-inspiring mystery. As we entered this temple of wisdom – which in truth was a cheap canvas tent set up by roadies the day before – there in all her splendor was Helga – at least her head. Our jaws dropped as we gazed upon the beautiful blonde head of Helga sitting in a box with mirrors all around her so that we could see there was no deception involved. My friends and I had a look at her for a few minutes before leaving – being too shy to ask her out on a date and slightly confused over the logistics of taking a head to dinner and a movie – in awe of this great human and perhaps even divine mystery.

After sampling a few more cheesy rides around the fairgrounds, we were still talking about Helga, and her head. We couldn't sort out how this mystery could possibly be. Someone suggested going back for another visit. As we approached the "Shrine de la Tête" for a second time, it seemed like something was different. The same voice came over the sound system. There was still no line-up, but as we entered the tent we suddenly came face to face with the truth. There was a new Head of Helga in the box, a brunette this time, and out behind the tent we could see "our" Helga from a couple hours ago having a smoke with a fully attached body! The great mystery of Helga was solved. We had been duped once again by another scam artist.

Skepticism is born from experiences like this one. It makes resisting God all the more easy. After all, our generation is used to hoaxes and disappointments. We have shared experiences like the Milli Vanilli scandal in music, the Monica Lewinski mess in politics, the Olympic Figure Skating judging fix in sports, an unbelievably long list of TV evangelists falling off their pedestals, and even the whole joke they called Y2K in technology. As a result, it takes quite a bit to shock us and quite a bit more to impress us.

This includes issues of faith that many of us left behind in the days when Santa Claus and the Easter bunny were cruelly revealed as hoaxes. As many of our childhood belief systems began to break down in those tumultuous teen years, God was often the first to go. Many people have their own "Head of Helga" experiences that lead them to questions like these:

- "Is there really a God?"
- "Is it all a hoax?"
- "Is God really just people's overactive imagination of a disembodied voice floating around the room?"
- "Even if we think there might be a God, what happens when we go on a couple of rides in our life and then come back? Is God still there and does God look the same?"

Such questions often lead to serious doubt, skepticism, and eventually a full-blown resistance to the idea of God.

Wandering from God

Without the slightest hint of regret, we Gen Xers leave behind our childhood faith and pursue our lives in the world. Like a North American rite of passage, those of us actually raised in a church often go through the rite called "confirmation" as a teenager (known more accurately to most as "graduation" from the childishness of Sunday school classes) and our active religious lives come to an end.

As our "real education" begins in the world, we seek degrees, jobs, relationships, new DVD players, a reliable car, and a decent apartment or condo to call home. Sunday mornings quickly and easily become the only day of the week we can sleep in. Church becomes only a place to show up for family weddings, funerals, and the odd Christmas Eve service.

To us, God seems like a preoccupation for people who are sitting in nursing homes waiting to die. Instead, as self-made women and men like Jacob, we prefer to pop open our favorite cooler or beer, stretch out on the couch, and say, "Welcome to the good life…."

Three friends

For many Gen Xers "resistance to God" is a commonly held "belief." To help me better understand the variety of resistance to God that exists in our Gen X age group, I gathered together three friends and asked them about their beliefs. Maybe you will identify with one of them.

Jeff, 32 years old, architect

Jeff was raised in a home where no one went to church. Neighbors and friends who did go were known as sentimental at best and nutty the rest of the time when they tried to talk about their faith. As Jeff put it, "We thought of them like the Dixie Chicks would say, square people in a world that's round." Their beliefs and practices were often regarded as superstitious and silly. For Jeff, the language of God and the symbols of the church are as foreign as liver spots. His only encounter with Christianity is someone trying to proselytize him on a street corner, or maybe catching the odd TV evangelist every now and then when flipping channels on a Sunday morning.

Sara, 26 years old, English teacher

Sara was raised in a Roman Catholic home and forced to go to church, catechism, and other childhood events associated with formation in the Catholic church. In the process she lost all her respect for priests, describing them today as "creepy." She found church a terrible bore and a complete waste of time. Now, she almost feels a sense of pity towards those who are shamed into going because of their "Catholic conscience" based on guilt. She comes close to active hostility in her attitudes towards her former church. She feels that it fundamentally failed her in issues of identity, meaning, sexuality, relationships, and spiritual beliefs. The language of God, symbols of the church, and other "churchy" things just bring back bad memories and create negative feelings.

Craig, 24 years old, college student

Craig was raised in a Protestant home and went to a local mainline Protestant church. Although he thinks of the church as a kind and happy place, he doesn't think it has much to do with his life at this time. In the future, if and when he gets married, he will probably do so in the church and will bring his kids for baptism later in life – but mostly to please his parents. He shows a great deal of respect for people in "ordained ministry," has a fondness for the church, and yet only shows up occasionally at Christmas Eve or Easter morning services. The language of God and the symbols of the church are friendly childhood reminders of a simpler time, perhaps best described as a time of innocence.

Living in spiritual poverty

Of course, if this was all there was to say on the subject then skepticism and resistance to God would win the day – end of story. What I have found, however, and what you may have felt yourself, is that there is a yearning for something deeper within our Generation X than just meets the eye.

Indeed, I find it curious to watch those around me, in their twenties and thirties, who struggle morning, noon and night with becoming "successful." You know the sort of lifestyle that I'm talking about – to land a job that is powerful and coveted by others, to work hard and make lots of money, while still having time to make it home in time to cut the grass, make the dinner, and relax with a good TV program at night. And my friends and colleagues are succeeding in attaining those goals. But I find that once they reach those higher levels of power in business, law, politics, education and so on, they are often left with an empty feeling and a big hole at the center of their lives. This feeling may be expressed by thoughts like "Is this all there is to life?"; "Why am I here?"; "Now that I have everything, why is this still not enough?"

Believe it or not, this feeling of emptiness is the first crack in the armor of our resistance to God. The reminder of the spiritual poverty affecting our generation came to me from a fellow Gen Xer named Daniel.

I met Daniel on a mission trip one summer to a remote part of northwestern Kenya to visit a church-run refugee camp. Daniel was a tall, handsome guy whose eyes betrayed the horrors of violence and suffering that too many people had experienced in this forgotten corner of the world. Daniel's home – properly called the Kakuma refugee camp – is a makeshift holding center for over 80,000 homeless souls desperate to return from where they came but instead forced to scratch out a living in that desolate place due to war, famine, and political/religious persecution.

In our stay at the camp we encountered a large group of teenage refugees dubbed by the western media "The Lost Boys of Sudan." Daniel was one of them.

This group of young men and teenage boys fled their homes in the middle of the world's longest civil war, a war that has left over two million dead in the last 18 years alone.[2] In 1987 when fighting intensified in southern Sudan, 5,000 boys fled the region on foot – first to Ethiopia, and then when that region destabilized too they walked all the way on to Kenya in 1992. The majority of these minors had lost all contact with their families. Most of their parents had been killed in the fighting or lost during their desperate flight from the region.[3] Our small mission team of young adults from The United Church of Canada listened to their stories of growing up in a culture of violence. We heard about their personal struggle to survive and about the faith in God that kept them going.

---

[2] *The Scorched Earth: Oil and War in Sudan* by Christian Aid (London: Russell Press, 2001) p. 5.

[3] *2000 Annual Report of The Lutheran World Federation/Department for World Service's Kenya/Sudan Programme* (Makuyu: Don Bosco Printing Press, 2001).

Their stories were both moving and humbling to me. They awakened a sense of unearned privilege in my own life, for having been lucky enough to be born in such a wealthy and generally peaceful nation like Canada.

Later that day I entered the "church" at Kakuma refugee camp to reflect on the stories I'd heard and to try to write down some of those stories before the names and faces began to fade from memory. The "church" was an open space with mud pews and large trees in the middle of the sanctuary whose trunks resembled the giant stone pillars in a European Cathedral. The branches of these trees reached upwards toward heaven and their leaves provided shelter to those who gathered below. I sat underneath one of these trees on a mud pew and opened my journal.

I scribbled as many of the names and stories of the people that I could remember and felt the depth of their emotion. As I wrote their story I was reminded of God's story with the people of Israel recorded in scripture, where they cried out after their city of Jerusalem had been sacked and people scattered. While centuries and generations had passed between their time and ours, the emotion recorded in the book of Lamentations could easily describe so many in today's world who suffer in a culture of violence and oppression:

> *Is it nothing to you, all you who pass by?*
> *Look and see if there is any sorrow like my sorrow.*
> *My eyes are spent with weeping; my stomach churns;*
> *my bile is poured out on the ground*
> *because of the destruction of my people,*
> *because infants and babes faint in the streets of the city.* [4]

When we come face to face with this kind of suffering it's hard not to ask, "In this world that we're living in, is there anything sacred?"

---

[4] Lamentations 1:12a, 2:11, *New Revised Standard Version* (Nashville: Nelson, by permission of the National Council of the Churches of Christ in the U.S.A., 1989).

Is there anything sacred?

In the midst of such suffering and sadness I had not expected to encounter the sacred. And yet I was filled with awe at the faith these young people had in God despite all they had experienced. In my journal I recalled Daniel's voice. After sharing his painful and tragic story, he concluded by saying "After all I've been through I still believe in God – and God is good."

I paused briefly from recording Daniel's story. In the margin of my journal scribbled "2 Corinthians 4:8-10," because generations before Christians had echoed Daniel's trust and confidence when they proclaimed

We are afflicted in every way, but not crushed; perplexed, but not driven to despair; persecuted, but not forsaken; struck down, but not destroyed; always carrying in the body the death of Jesus, so that the life of Jesus may also be made visible in our bodies. [5]

[5] 2 Corinthians 4:8-10. *New Revised Standard Version* (Nashville: Nelson, by permission of the National Council of the Churches of Christ in the U.S.A., 1989).

I remember Daniel straightening up and adding one last fascinating thought. "You know," he said to me with concerned eyes, "we get a lot of magazines donated to us here from North America. And what frustrates me the most is how North Americans always portray us as being in a state of poverty. But you know, when I look at North American culture I just see spiritual poverty."

I was amazed that after all these people had been through they still had such a solid faith – and ashamed that when they looked at our privileged North American backgrounds they felt pity at our spiritual shallowness. I was reminded of how Jesus said that he was sent so that humankind might have life and have it abundantly. [6]

For many in our generation abundant life or "the good life" has always meant achieving positions of power, possessions of great value, and doing it on your own. But what happens if after time this simply is not enough? Is it possible that the definition of the good life may have to be revised to include something we've been resisting for a long time?

[6] John 10:10.

Periodically, through this book, I am going to put in some questions that you might pause to think about.

If you're reading this book by yourself, I suggest you just sit back and reflect on these questions. You might make some notes on a sheet of paper – writing things down forces you to be more concrete, more precise. Writing out your responses makes it harder for you to be satisfied with easy answers.

If you and some others are working through this book together, like a study group, you could use these questions as a means of getting discussion going. The idea of the questions is to help you sort out what you really think, not to come to some kind of premature agreement. In such a discussion, be respectful of the variety of experiences present and remain open-minded to those stories very different from your own.

Questions for reflection

- What do you resist doing in your life? Doing the laundry, going to the dentist, studying or assignments at work...?
- What would happen if you never addressed these concerns and let them go indefinitely?
- Would it be a huge stretch to include spirituality on this list? What do you think happens if you resist thinking or talking about spirituality indefinitely?
- Can you relate to The Head of Helga story? How much does skepticism help you resist thinking about spirituality?
- Has your image of what God is like changed much from childhood? If you were to draw a picture of your idea of God, what would it look like? How would it be different from your earliest ideas about God?

2

Rediscovering God

Jacob left Beersheba and went to Haran. He came to a certain place and camped for the night since the sun had set. He took one of the stones there, set it under his head and lay down to sleep. And he dreamed: A stairway was set on the ground and it reached all the way to the sky; angels of God were going up and down on it. Then God was right before him, saying "I am God, the God of Abraham your father and the God of Isaac. I'm giving the ground on which you are sleeping to you and to your descendants. Your descendants will be as the dust of the Earth; they'll stretch from west to east and from north to south. All the families of the Earth will bless themselves in you and your descendants. Yes. I'll stay with you, I'll protect you wherever you go, and I'll bring back to this very ground. I'll stick with you until I've done everything I promised you."

Jacob woke up from his sleep. He said, "God is in this place – truly. And I didn't even know it!" He was terrified. He whispered in awe, "Incredible. Wonderful. Holy. This is God's House. This is the Gate of Heaven." [1]

When I left Jacob in the last chapter, he was living the good life and looking out for number one. After a while, however, his "me first" lifestyle started to tick people off. He eventually had to leave home, afraid that his own brother wanted to kill him.

It is at this time, when his life is unsettled, his direction unclear, that God comes crashing into Jacob's life without warning. Suddenly, his skepticism and his resistance to his parents' and grandparents' religion melts away as he tries to sleep in a cold

---

[1] Genesis 28:10-17, *The Message: The Bible in Contemporary Language,* by Eugene H. Peterson (Colorado Springs: NavPress, 1993).

and desolate place. In the darkness, he senses that he is not alone, after all. He stands before God.

Jacob responds by waking and declaring, "Surely the Lord is in this place – and I did not know it! How awesome is this place!"

Awesome, indeed. For Jacob has gone from resisting God most of his young adult years to rediscovering God active in his life.

The same thing is happening to many Gen Xers today – even though they may not face as threatening a situation as Jacob did. Between a slumping economy, the risks of terrorism, and the potential for wars, many are feeling the foundations of their lives falling apart. And like Jacob, they are rediscovering God.

Now, I say *rediscovering* God because I believe that we are loving creations shaped by the Creator and have at our beginning known God. Of course, as we grow we are shaped by our culture; often we have been given unhelpful images of God that dominate our impression of the divine. We need to unlearn those images from our Sunday schools of God as an old man with a white beard sitting on a cloud, like something from a Far Side cartoon. These images may have been suitable for our age and maturity back then, but they no longer suit our situation. Since those years, we have grown up. So should our ideas about God.

God rediscovered throughout history

Throughout time God has tried various methods to be revealed to humankind. God has been there all along, waiting with eager anticipation to be rediscovered by women and men throughout the world. Sometimes these discoveries are dramatic, like Jacob encountering God in his dream with the ladder. Sometimes they're quite ordinary.

The New Testament records another famous "rediscovery" of God through Saul, a guy who really had it in for Christians. Unlike Jacob, Saul thought he already knew God. He was a Jewish rabbi, a scholar at the Temple in Jerusalem who had developed a hatred for these new Christian troublemakers. As the Acts of the Apostles records

All this time Saul was breathing down the necks of the

Master's disciples, out for the kill. He went to the Chief Priest and got arrest warrants to take to the meeting places in Damascus so that if he found anyone there belonging to the Way, whether men or women, he could arrest them and bring them to Jerusalem.

He set off. When he got to the outskirts of Damascus, he was suddenly dazed by a blinding flash of light. As he fell to the ground, he heard a voice: "Saul, Saul, why are you out to get me?"

He said, "Who are you, Master?

"I am Jesus, the One you're hunting down. I want you to get up and enter the city. In the city you'll be told what to do next." [2]

After this encounter, Saul changes his identity to Paul. He goes on to be known as Saint Paul, and to have an overwhelming number of churches, schools, towns, and hockey rinks named after him.

[2] Acts 9:1-6, *The Message: The Bible in Contemporary Language,* by Eugene H. Peterson (Colorado Springs: NavPress, 1993).

And it all began in the rediscovering of God in his life.

Don't let these two stories, of Paul and Jacob, suggest that God was finished revealing the divine nature or that God was only rediscovered by humankind in the biblical times. Right through history, God has been active creating, redeeming and sustaining the world and all its inhabitants, hoping to be rediscovered by God's children.

If Paul's blinding-light rediscovery is a bit much for you, perhaps a more subtle but equally famous rediscovery of God as found in the story of John Wesley will help.

John Wesley was an ordained priest in the Anglican Church who was at times as poor at being a minister as William Shatner is at acting. Wesley's early ministry years were a disaster, with one particularly bad stay in Georgia (then still a British colony) where he ministered to settlers. At some point he fell in love with a member of his church, but when she decided to marry someone else he was furious and ruined her good name in the community. Her uncle, who happened to be an expert in law, sued the pants off John Wesley. Wesley turned tail and ran back to England. At this point in his life, he wrote in his journal

I went to America to convert the Indians but, oh, who shall convert me?

Yet it was at this lowest point in his life that John Wesley rediscovered God. A short time after returning to England, Wesley showed up at a small religious gathering.

In the evening, I went very unwillingly to a society in Aldersgate Street, where one was reading Luther's Preface to the Epistle to the Romans. About a quarter before nine, while he was describing the change which God works in the heart through faith in Christ, I felt my heart strangely warmed. *I felt I did trust in Christ, Christ alone for salvation…*

After John struggled for so long, God finally got through to him and transformed his life. Wesley caught fire. He began preaching at any church that would have him, and when many churches closed their doors, he went out into the fields and the market places of England. To nurture his new converts, he devised a "method" of incorporating them into little communities or cells of faithful Christians. He would go on to build a Christian community so strong that it spread throughout the world, forming churches in many new places. Eventually, the churches he founded were called Methodist churches, and they included the largest church that joined to form The United Church of Canada in 1925.

Deep fryer faith or slow cooker belief?

St. Paul and John Wesley highlight two different approaches to rediscovering God. One is unexpected and quick; the other is a slow and painful journey of searching before finding some small measure of discovery. With Paul it was like his heart and mind were thrown into the deep fryer at McDonald's and came out two minutes later golden brown and ready to serve (to serve God, that is!). Wesley, on the other hand, had a heart and mind that needed some time in the slow cooker for the stew of his life to develop its full flavor.

Both stories are valid and important, but I have a feeling that the majority of us rediscover God in more of a slow "warming of the heart" way like Wesley, as opposed to a bolt of lightning experience from heaven. For many, our faith simmers over a number of years before we can authentically be plucked out of the pot and called a "new creation."

God on the dance floor

Think of it this way. It is entirely possible for two people to meet in Las Vegas, fall in love, and get married that very day, right? And some of them even live happily ever after. But most of us, before we are willing to make a lifelong commitment like marriage, want to date someone for a while to get to know them. In the same way, some people meet God and want to get married right away. The rest of us, however, need some time to date God and to get to know God better before we can make that decision.

Of course, the exciting news is that God is always the one who asks us out on the first date. In fact, God's ongoing invitation to humankind can be likened to the subtle act of simply asking for a dance...

If someone were to write the story of God's courtship of humankind, an appropriate setting might just be a hot smoky nightclub on the edge of a university campus. In fact, you could probably better imagine the story if you put yourself in God's shoes. Imagine with me:

You enter a crowded dance club, decked out in your new GAP outfit, look around at the great mix of people gathered and head over to the bar for a drink. After standing and leaning against the bar sipping your drink for a few minutes, you muster up the courage to go over and ask someone to dance. Being a classy sort of person, you go over and introduce yourself – avoiding cheesy pickup lines like "If I told you that you had a great body, would hold it against me?" or "You know baby, the best thing that would look good on you is me!" (At all costs you avoid the worst pickup line of all time: "Does this look infected to you?")

Instead, you simply ask, "Would you like to dance?"

Much to your embarrassment, the response comes quickly and in the negative. The person you invited to dance stands up and walks away to another part of the nightclub.

Shaken, you turn and spot another potential partner. This time you ask with a little less confidence, "Do you want to dance?" Again the response comes quickly – another firm "No," followed by, "I'm waiting for something better to come along," which brings a burst of laughter from a tableful of friends sitting nearby.

Recoiling from this encounter, you muster up whatever courage you have left and turn to one last prospect, asking with great hesitation, "How 'bout a dance?"

Once again, imagine that the response is negative, with the added bonus of a drink being splashed in your face and all over your new outfit. Crushed, you recoil into the corner of the bar and try to make sense of what just happened.

Okay, I know that might never happen to you in the real world. But staying in character for a moment, think about how this encounter would make you feel. Rejected, hurt, humiliated, disillusioned, self-conscious, depressed? Well, believe it or not, now you know how God feels. Yes, God almighty, maker of heaven and earth, gets rejected *all the time*. So get rid of that silly Sunday school image of God as a big old white bearded man on a cloud, and start imagining God shuffling around a nightclub dance floor being turned down time and time again.

One of the most amazing things that this image reveals to us about God is that God could very easily turn away from all humans after being rejected time and time again. Yet, the story of God and humankind is an unending attempt by God to have us join the dance and be whisked out onto the dance floor. Instead of kindling anger against those who rejected him, God has bent over backwards to try new and exciting ways to ask the question, "Would you like to dance?"

Sometimes the question comes in a shocking way. God said to Jacob, "Jacob, if you decide to dance with me, I'll take care of you and stay with you through thick and thin." To St. Paul, God said, "I think it's time you made a change in your life and stopped hurting so many people around you. I can help make that happen you know – you and me together." And to John Wesley, in a still small voice, barely audible over the cacophony of other speakers, God said, "John, you've been searching for me for so long, isn't it time you let your heart lead for a while instead of your head?"

God continues to try different ways of engaging us today. God asks the question, "Would you like to dance with me through life?" differently to every generation and to every person. Yet, the choice always remains in our hands. Will we continue to reject God and follow the lead of others? Or will we leave our drink and our tableful of friends, grab God's hand, and head out onto the crowded dance floor to party like never before?

The homecoming

Jesus told his followers a story that highlights God's longing to reach out and be acknowledged by humankind.

There was once a man who had two sons. The younger said to his father, "Father, I want right now what's coming to me."

So the father divided the property between them. It wasn't long before the younger son packed his bags and left for a distant country. There, undisciplined and dissipated, he wasted everything he had. After he had gone through all his money, there was a bad famine all through that country and he began to hurt. He signed on with a citizen there who assigned him to his fields to slop the pigs. He was so hungry he would have eaten the corncobs in the pig slop, but no one would give him any.

That brought him to his senses. He said, "All those farmhands working for my father sit down to three meals a day, and here I am starving to death. I'm going back to my father, I'll say to him, "Father, I've sinned against God, I've sinned before you; I don't deserve to be called your son. Take me on as a hired hand." He got right up and went home to his father.

When he was still a long way off, his father saw him. His heart pounding, he ran out, embraced him and kissed him. The son started his speech: "Father, I've sinned against God,

I've sinned before you, I don't deserve to be called your son ever again."

But the father wasn't listening. He was calling to the servants. "Quick. Bring a clean set of clothes and dress him. Put the family ring on his finger and sandals on his feet. Then get a grain-fed heifer and roast it. We're going to feast! We're going to have a wonderful time! My son is here – given up for dead and now alive! Given up for lost and now found!" And they began to have a wonderful time. [3]

Jesus' story highlights the relief and joy felt by both father and child at their mutual rediscovery. God too rejoices when we give up resisting the urge to return home. Like the generous father, God runs towards us with arms extended wide, eager to embrace us. The resistance is over, the rediscovery complete, but the relationship has just begun. The son returning to his father's farm will now have to carve out a new existence back home.

[3] Luke 15:11-24, *The Message: The Bible in Contemporary Language,* by Eugene H. Peterson (Colorado Springs: NavPress, 1993).

It won't be long until that embrace turns into more of a clutch and grab as we wrestle with how to live faithfully with God. This struggle, you'll soon see, changed Jacob's life. That's the next challenge…

Questions for reflection

- What kind of life events have you experienced that made you question whether there was anything beyond this world or this life?
- Did the terrorist actions of September 11 stir any yearnings or questions about God? Do you expect life to be fair?
- What do you find more personally convincing – a deep fryer faith like Paul or a slow cooker faith like John Wesley? Which one might be more likely for you based on your own experience?
- How does the image of someone getting turned down while asking people to dance change your impressions of God?
- What feeling(s) does the story of the father welcoming back the long-lost child evoke in you? How would you respond to a father who welcomed you back with open arms? Can you imagine God welcoming you back with open arms?

3

Relationship with God

Jacob had a rediscovery experience. After some difficult years in exile, he had to escape again. But he had only one place left that he could go – back home, back to where he believed his older brother still wanted to kill him. He came to the boundary of his brother's territory, and got scared.

But during the night (Jacob) got up and took his (family)…
and crossed the ford of the Jabbok. He got them safely across
the brook along with all his possessions.
But Jacob stayed behind by himself, and a man wrestled

with him until daybreak. When the man saw that he couldn't get the best of Jacob as they wrestled, he deliberately threw Jacob's hip out of joint.

The man said, "Let me go; it's daybreak."

Jacob said, "I'm not letting you go 'til you bless me."

The man said, "What's your name?"

He answered, "Jacob."

The man said, "But no longer. Your name is no longer Jacob. From now on it's Israel (which means God-wrestler); you've wrestled with God and you've come through." [1]

Once again heaven touches earth for Jacob. But this time, instead of being a passive observer, Jacob is fully engaged with God. Jacob wrestles a mysterious stranger identified throughout history as a man, an angel, or God in person. Jacob discovers that life beyond rediscovering God will not be easy, but through the struggle he receives the promise that his life and his very identity

[1] Genesis 32:22-32, *The Message: The Bible in Contemporary Language,* by Eugene H. Peterson (Colorado Springs: NavPress, 1993).

will be transformed. As Jacob's knowledge and experience of God increase, he moves from merely rediscovering God to a rich new relationship with the Creator.

This path of rediscovering, of moving towards a new and richer relationship, continues today between the Almighty and humankind.

Bumping God's table

Some of my favorite childhood memories are of time spent up at our family cottage just outside Kenora in northwestern Ontario. On the warm and sunny days, my cousins and I would swim, canoe, and water-ski until the sun went down. But of course, anyone who has a cottage knows the greatest dilemma comes on the cold rainy days when you have to entertain a cottage full of bored children.

In these periods of boredom, my diversion of choice was not reading a book or playing a board game. Rather, I spent my free time building card houses. Taking old decks of playing cards I found around the cottage, I would start simple, making a little bungalow for myself. The simple house, however, would soon turn into a rather grand subdivision of card houses, followed by a sports arena, shopping mall, airport, and so forth, until the entire kitchen table was filled with a card city. Indeed, in a rather undemocratic move, I even elected myself mayor of this fast-growing card city!

Then, without fail, someone in my family would come in from the rainy day outside and bang the big old back door that shook the very frame of the cottage itself. In a flash, pillar upon pillar collapsed. Within seconds I went from mayor of the greatest card city of all time to a teary-eyed little boy surrounded by jacks, queens, kings, and aces scattered all over the floor. Nothing was left standing.

Today, a little older and perhaps a wee bit wiser, I can't help noticing some strong similarities between my generation's search for a meaningful relationship with God and that small-boy experience. It seems to me that we spend a great deal of time in life constructing our own reality quite apart from God's input. Our card-house lives may look fine from the outside but they are in great danger of collapsing at any moment. Indeed, when we go from resisting God to rediscovering God, it is just like that back door slamming and all the cards collapsing in an instant. God's entry into our lives sweeps away all our preconceived notions of what to build our lives on, and shakes the meaning of life to its very foundation. It is an exciting and sometimes frightening prospect, since our foundations are revealed as cracked and in need of repair.

Matthew, one of Jesus' followers, wrote a biography of Jesus in which he recorded his Master's teaching on the foundation of faith. Jesus' words take on new significance in the context of card houses:

These words I speak to you are not incidental additions to your life, homeowner improvements to your standard of living. They are foundational words, words to build your life on. If you work these words into your life, you are like a smart carpenter who built his house on solid rock. Rain poured down, the river flooded, a tornado hit – but nothing moved that house. It was fixed to rock.

But if you just use my words in Bible studies and don't work them into your life, you are like a stupid carpenter who built his house on the sandy beach. When a storm rolled in and the waves came up, it collapsed like a house of cards. [2]

Jesus' message both comforts and challenges us. You see, after resisting God and rediscovering the Divine, our cards are lying flat on the table, scattered around us. Now we have to decide how to live every day in the world. We live after discovering God in danger of reconstructing our card-house life on another shaky foundation. After we have danced a little with God we may be tempted to break it off and return to our seats on the edge of the dance floor. Jesus' story highlights the need for us to move beyond merely rediscovering God to a long-term relationship with God. Jesus reminds us that our foundation of faith must be one as firm as rock – built on the rock of ages.

[2] Matthew 7:24-27, *The Message: The Bible in Contemporary Language,* by Eugene H. Peterson (Colorado Springs: NavPress, 1993).

Jesus the signpost of God

But Jesus is troubling for many people. They don't know what to make of him.

Talking about Jesus in depth is often a daunting and difficult prospect. A great many people in relationship with God shy away from talking publicly about their faith. Instead, the only ones left to talk about Jesus are people confronting strangers on street corners, handing out leaflets on buses and subways, or storming around on TV shouting out demons and using bizarre expressions like "Have you been saved by the blood of the lamb?" These are the same kind of folks who are fond of sporting bumper stickers like "JESUS IS THE ANSWER" while the rest of us are left scratching our heads and asking each other, "What was the question?"

Yet relationship with God is inseparable from life as a follower of Jesus. So who is Jesus?

We know that Jesus was both a gift from God and a gift of God himself. In short, Jesus is the signpost to God. Think of it this way.

Have you ever experienced that unmistakable feeling of being trapped on a long highway with a full bladder in the middle of winter? How does it feel? For me, it was an all too familiar feeling on the countless trips I have made between my childhood home in Winnipeg to visit friends and family in Calgary, across the frozen pond we affectionately know and love as Saskatchewan. Inevitably, halfway across the province in the middle of nowhere, my bladder set off alarm bells. At this point, to the great alarm of my traveling companions, I announce, "If my bladder were a battleship, it would be on RED ALERT!" As the kilometers roll by, I begin to float out of my seat.

Fortunately, just before I begin to consider the advantages of wearing Depends, someone from the front seat shouts with great delight, "Look at that sign straight ahead." As I lean forward in my seat (not too quickly now) I see salvation and shout with joy, "I know that my bladder liveth," to paraphrase Handel's *Messiah,* for in the distance is a sign pointing towards a truck stop, gas station, fast food restaurant, or some other place where I can empty my bladder before I have to disgrace myself.

Well, believe it or not, Jesus continues to be something like that crude example for all of humanity. Jesus serves as a signpost pointing people towards God – the Creator of all things – the place to go (not quite so literally) to relieve (again not so literally) all of our concerns and fears. Jesus points towards the One who gives meaning and purpose to our lives and reminds us how much we are loved by the Creator. This message of hope is why Christians describe Jesus' message in the Bible as "Good News."

Who's your daddy?

On study breaks at seminary, I often cleared my mind by wandering downstairs to the common room, to view a little trash TV. Trash talk shows always manage to keep my attention despite how ridiculous they get. One show that sticks out in my mind was entitled, "Who's your daddy?" On this day, the guests were all pregnant but absolutely stymied as to who the father was since they had slept with so many different guys. Of course, in the next step, the host invited out all the potential fathers. The show climaxed (if you'll forgive one more pun) in the public proclamation of paternity tests within the last ten minutes of the show.

In a much more dignified way, Jesus revealed a paternity test of his own during his short life on earth. He reveals that God is his Father and indeed the Father of all humanity. The proof comes not in DNA testing but in personality, essence, and action – Jesus mirrors the nature of God too accurately to be unrelated. This revelation speaks directly to our move from resisting God and then rediscovering God, to a relationship with God. We go from an unknown relationship to becoming children of God.

From resistance to rejection of Jesus

Of course, the threefold pattern of resisting, rediscovering, and relationship with God is nothing new. It existed in Jesus' day as well. As Jesus taught his radical message of God's great love for all humankind he often undermined the political and social framework, the card-house construction of power in 1st-century Palestine. As a result, it seemed that for every person who heard Jesus' message of love and justice and rediscovered God, there were ten more who resisted God. And for every person who responded to the divine invitation of relationship with God that Jesus delivered, there were another hundred who left in a huff and resisted God. The result was that Jesus made a really large number of enemies in his short number of years living with us.

In the end, those who resisted God clearly outnumbered those who rediscovered God and those who built a relationship with God. It also helped that those who resisted God also held the political, economic, and military power of Jesus' context. The decision was simple for them – eliminate the leader and scatter the followers.

So Jesus was arrested, beaten, and sentenced to death on trumped up charges of sedition against the state. And if you were hoping for some Chuck Norris style Delta Force rescue by Jesus' disciples, you'll be sorely disappointed. The disciples, having rediscovered God and begun a new relationship with God through Jesus, were paralyzed by fear and abandoned Jesus.

And so, on a bleak and crisp Friday morning, Jesus joined a procession of other criminals up to a hill soaked in the blood of previous executions. He was given the ancient world's equivalent of the electric chair. If he'd been in Texas, they'd have broadcast it on the 6 o'clock news. Jesus was nailed to a rough cross with his flesh pierced at the wrists and feet. Jesus, the Son of God, suffered a slow and horrible death, crying out in pain and choking on the fluids filling his lungs in the scorching heat of the Palestinian sun. As Jesus suffered, God grieved. It seemed that resistance to God had won the day.

And yet, that same God who revealed himself to Jacob in a dream and wrestled with him till daybreak was there beside Jesus. That same God who changed the course of St. Paul's life in a blinding flash of light was there within Jesus. That same God who warmed the withered heart of the disillusioned John Wesley and nurtured growth in faith was there above Jesus. That same God who continues to cross the dance floor and invite you and me to a dance of faith was there in Jesus and was about to make the greatest dance move the world had ever seen.

In a terrible act of selfish arrogance, humankind poured out its scorn, its anger and its disbelief in the act of crucifying Jesus.

It was as if humankind had said to God, "Hey God, if Jesus is the best you could send us, what are you going to do now?"

In a still, small voice God answered, "Just watch me."

And in an act of loving kindness that continues to irritate skeptics, baffle historians, challenge theologians, and comfort Christians, God's answer was to overcome humankind's worst evil with a simple act of love. God stooped over the cold, rigid body of Jesus and let a solitary tear fall from the divine face. You can almost imagine God whispering in a shaky voice, full of grief not rage,

> *My love for you is greater than all their hate and fear combined. My love for all humankind is greater than they could ever know or understand. By your death, they revealed the depth of their unjust and callous hearts. Now, by your new life, may my children know the warmth of a Father's love. Come, my beloved Son, be filled with the Spirit's power and live again. We have much work to do....*

And so, on the third day, when two female disciples of Jesus went to visit his grave, they discovered the true depth of God's love. As one of the biographies of Jesus records,

After the Sabbath, as the first light of the new week dawned, Mary Magdalene and the other Mary came to keep vigil at the tomb. Suddenly the earth reeled and rocked under their feet as God's angel came down from heaven, came right up to where they were standing. He rolled back the stone and then sat on it. Shafts of lightning blazed from him. His garments shimmered snow-white. The guards at the tomb were scared to death. They were so frightened, they couldn't move.

The angel spoke to the women: "There is nothing to fear here. I know you're looking for Jesus, the One they nailed to the cross. He is not here. He was raised, just as he said. Come

and look at the place where he was placed.

"Now, get on your way quickly and tell his disciples, 'He is risen from the dead. He is going on ahead of you to Galilee. You will see him there.' That's the message." [3]

And as the women turned and ran to tell the others, the Christian church was born. God's relationship with humankind would never be the same again.

The Holy Spirit, God's courier service

After Jesus' disciples heard about the amazing news of Jesus' resurrection, the Holy Spirit began to play a bigger role in the story of the early Christian Church. Don't get me wrong – the Holy Spirit was active throughout history and is in the Bible in other places, but it just gets a lot more air time in the story of the

---

[3] Matthew 28:1-7, *The Message: The Bible in Contemporary Language,* by Eugene H. Peterson (Colorado Springs: NavPress, 1993).

first days of the church. For example, before Jesus is murdered he gave a hint of the Holy Spirit's active role in the early church when he said,

> *I'm telling you these things while I'm still living with you. The Friend, the Holy Spirit whom the Father will send at my request, will make everything plain to you. He will remind you of all things I have told you. I'm leaving you well and whole. That's my parting gift to you. Peace. I don't leave you the way you're used to being left – feeling abandoned, bereft. So don't be upset. Don't be distraught.* [4]

Jesus, always true to his word, sends the Holy Spirit at one of the first meetings between the risen Jesus and his followers.

> *Meanwhile, the eleven disciples were on their way to Galilee, headed for the mountain Jesus had set for their reunion. The*

[4] John 14:25-27, *The Message: The Bible in Contemporary Language,* by Eugene H. Peterson (Colorado Springs: NavPress, 1993).

moment they saw him they worshiped him. Some, though, held back, not sure about worship, about risking themselves totally.

Jesus, undeterred, went right ahead and gave his charge: "God authorized and commanded me to commission you: Go out and train everyone you meet, far and near, in this way of life, marking them by baptism in the threefold name: Father, Son and Holy Spirit. Then instruct them in the practice of all I have commanded you. I'll be with you as you do this, day after day after day, right up to the end of the age." [5]

So who or what is this Holy Spirit? Based on the testimony of Jesus and the early church, the Spirit is God's active agent in the world. It is the Spirit of God who reveals wisdom to followers of Jesus, inspires them to acts of loving kindness against injustice around them, comforts them in times of sadness, and reminds them they

---

[5] Matthew 28:16-20, *The Message: The Bible in Contemporary Language,* by Eugene H. Peterson (Colorado Springs: NavPress, 1993).

are not alone. The Holy Spirit acts as the courier for those of us who pray/talk to God, relaying messages between humankind and God our Creator.

No assembly required

Now this may start to sound a little confusing. Good – you're not alone. The relationship between Father, Son, and Holy Spirit has been studied enough to fill endless bookcases with doctoral dissertations, sermon collections, and diary musings. The one thing the Trinity (God the Father, Son, Holy Spirit) is not is a do-it-yourself God.

Have you ever bought one of those packaged kits for a barbecue or a kid's wagon from Canadian Tire, or almost anything from IKEA, that comes in five million pieces and warns you "Some assembly required"? I know the greatest test of my first days of marriage was assembling countless IKEA products with that frustrating little hexagonal wrench. Well, rest assured God the Father, Son, and Holy Spirit is not a kit you have to put together yourself. The Divine requires no IKEA wrench or instructions printed in Swedish! The most basic understanding of the Trinity is that, based on the biographies of Jesus and the history of the early church, God is known in three distinct yet united ways. The Divine is revealed to humankind as the Living God, Risen Christ, and Loving Spirit. Ever since the early days of the church, Christians have celebrated this unique revelation of God that deepens as we enter into relationship with God. As the early church sang and we still do today:

> *Glory be to the Father, and to the Son,*
> *And to the Holy Spirit.*
> *As it was in the beginning, is now and ever shall be,*
> *World without end. Amen.*

Therefore, just like in human relationships, as we move from rediscovering God to a relationship with God, we deepen our understanding of God's Divine nature. The life, death, and resurrection of Jesus illustrates God the Creator's overwhelming love for humankind, and the Holy Spirit is an ever-present agent in the world revealing God's actions and passion for you and me.

Getting to know God

So what does this all mean for you and me? How does this understanding of the "Threefold God" affect our relationship with God? For starters, it reveals more about who God is and how God relates to you and me. God exists in a community of mutual, self-giving love. This three-dimensional revelation of God means we can never be satisfied with simple single-minded perspectives, like a cardboard cutout God designed to fit into a single slot of life. For example, humankind's rejection and execution of Jesus was the ultimate test of God's love, patience, and compassion for humankind. Never before had God risked God's own self this way.

As the Creator of all things, God would have been justified in just "pulling the plug" on the human experiment, throwing up his hands and saying, "You see, I knew giving humans free will was a bad idea." Indeed, God did something very like that, a long time before, when God wiped out all humans except Noah and his family, in a gigantic flood. Instead, we now know through Jesus that God responded not in anger but in love. Christians sum up this amazing action in one simple word – grace. By grace I do not mean necessarily the rambling words uttered by Uncle Joe or Grandma at the Thanksgiving dinner table while the food is turning cold. Christians understand grace to mean that the depth of God's love made available to humankind through Jesus is a pure gift. As John Wesley described it, "an undeserved favor."

This free and freeing love of God is poured out liberally onto humankind like gravy poured out over that turkey and mashed potatoes at Thanksgiving dinner. Like a fine meal, of course, once you've tasted it you want more and more. And so, as we move from resisting God to rediscovering God and on to a relationship with God, we share a greater awareness with other Christians of this gift of grace.

There are some ways that we can direct our lives to better absorb this love of God as we continue to develop our relationship with the Almighty. Here are a couple of examples:

1. Praying attention to God

Prayer can often appear to those who are developing a relationship with God to be a rigid and unmoving experience. As kids in Sunday school we were taught to bow our heads, close our eyes, and listen to someone speak a few words, right? Well, forget that.

Prayer is not just empty words but a real communication with God the Father, Son, and Holy Spirit. Prayer is a conversation. It is our time to approach God and share our thoughts and concerns with our Creator. It should be as natural as sitting and chatting to a friend on the phone. So, sit however you like. Keep your eyes open, if that feels more natural.

Of course, like any good conversation with a friend, you need to be open to the other's concerns as well. So take the time to sit quietly for part of your conversation and listen for God. Don't worry if your mind wanders; God will meet you wherever you go.

To begin with, "praying attention" to your relationship with God can be as simple as saying words like

Hey God,
Thanks for being there for me because in a world that too often disappoints me, I know that you're always faithful. I screw up a lot but I really want you to help me figure out how to live my life.
Amen.

Some people like a little more structure to their conversation with God. Over the years various forms of prayer have been developed by Christians. One of the most basic forms is called a "collect," and you may find this a helpful guide to kick-start your prayer life.

Address	*O God,*
Attribute	*you are always faithful and loving to me.*
Petition	*Fill me with your wisdom and peace,*
Purpose	*so that I can get through this day.*
Closing	*Through Jesus Christ my Lord, Amen.*

Some prayers sound almost like poetry. Some of my favorites come from the Celtic tradition. The Celtic Christians of northern Europe, Britain, and Ireland have left us a wealth of conversation aids with our Divine Parent and encourage us to add to the list today. Celtic prayer was rooted in daily life and everyday concerns and was always deeply grounded in the Trinity of Father, Son, and Holy Spirit. Pray this prayer, for example:

The Trinity
The Trinity protecting me.
The Father be over me.
The Saviour be under me.
The Spirit be about me.
The Holy Three defending me.
As evening come bless my home.
Holy Three watching me.
As shadows fall hear my call.

Sacred Three encircle me.
So it may be.
Amen to Thee,
Holy Three about me.
Amen. [6]

As you further develop your relationship with God, communication is essential. After a while you'll find that prayer becomes like Peter Parker's "spider sense tingling." Praying becomes more natural, while listening for God's direction becomes almost intuitive. Try finding a time of day, or several times (such as first thing in the morning, lunchtime, or before you sleep), to take time to both speak and listen to God. May this exercise bring you peace and direction in your relationship with God.

---

[6] David Adam, *The Edge of Glory: Prayers in the Celtic Tradition* (Harrisburg: Morehouse Publishing, 1985) p. 9.

2. Getting to know God's story

As you continue to explore your relationship with God it would be helpful, in addition to communicating with God through prayer, if you took a little time to get to know God's story. This may have been the part you were dreading, but I can assure you there are ways to get to know God's story in the Bible that are not as painful as getting teeth pulled by Steve Martin playing a sadistic dentist in *Little Shop of Horrors*. I can also assure you that if you try to read the Bible cover to cover like any other book you will probably die and be eaten by vultures somewhere in one of the Old Testament sections like Leviticus or Numbers.

Instead, here are a few suggestions on how to most easily acquaint yourself with God's story:

- There are many different versions of the Bible at your local bookstore but try going for one of the newer translations. The *New Revised Standard Version* is probably the most authoritative, but other versions such as the *Good News Bible* or *The Message* that are written in contemporary English will be even easier to read.

- Begin by reading the stories of Jesus found in the biography (gospel) of Mark since it is the shortest of all the biographies on Jesus.

- You might want to move on to one of the letters that the early Christians wrote to one another that are found at the back of the New Testament, letters like 1 Corinthians, Galatians, or Ephesians, and "eavesdrop" on what the early Christians were saying about God and Jesus.

- At this point, try a few of the psalms found in the middle of the Bible. Psalms are actually song lyrics, so reading them is like scanning the inside jacket of a CD. A number of these songs are believed to have been written by King David. You'll find that they express all sorts of emotions, from joy to despair, as the writer communicates with God.

- Next, you may wish to try reading a bit through Genesis, the very beginning of the Bible, which contains the Judeo-

Christian story of how the world began. Don't be spooked into having to believe that these stories are "literally" true. Instead try to think of the message the author was trying to communicate, such as that God is the Creator of all life.

- For a healthy dose of God's vision of social justice, round off your introduction to the Bible with some of the prophets. Check out such amazing people of faith such as Joel, Micah, and Amos.

As you become more familiar with reading God's story of relationship with humankind you'll find that the Bible is not quite as boring as you first thought. In fact, I often imagine a Jerry Springer episode that would expose all the wacky characters and situations recorded in the scriptures. Take these Bible stories for example:

Sex (Genesis 4:1-2) –"Original Lov'n"
Adultery (2 Samuel 11) –"King David Pulls a Bill Clinton"
Incest (Genesis 19:30-38) –"Taking Dad on a Date"

Multiple partners (Genesis 16) –"Who Said the Ancient
   World Didn't Swing?"
Murder (Genesis 4:1-12) –"Brotherly Love?"
Overeating (Matthew 14:13-21) – "Jesus' All-you-can-eat
   Buffet"
WWE-style wrestling (Genesis 32:22-32) –"Jacob
   Wrestles the Angel and the Angel Takes a Cheap Shot"
Psychic insights (Genesis 41) –"Joseph Interprets Dreams"

Through prayer and through hearing God's story of reaching out
to humankind for relationship, you will find that God's story
will become intertwined with your own story. God's invitation
to relationship can help shape the direction and purpose of your
life by knowing who and whose you are. As Jesus said to all who
would listen,

*Are you tired? Worn out? Burned out on religion? Come to
me. Get away with me and you'll recover your life. I'll show
you how to take a real rest. Walk with me and work with me*

– watch how I do it. Learn the unforced rhythms of grace. I won't lay anything heavy or ill-fitting on you. Keep company with me and you'll learn to live freely and lightly. [7]

Jesus continues to invite those who would listen to join him in a life of prayer, study, and service that gives glory to God and meaning to our own lives. He invites us to the most glorious party possible – a life that resonates deeply with the unforced rhythms of God's grace. This is the gift and joy that relationship with God brings.

[7] Matthew 11:28-30, *The Message: The Bible in Contemporary Language,* by Eugene H. Peterson (Colorado Springs: NavPress, 1993).

Questions for reflection

- List some characteristics of the personality of Jesus, as you know him. Now list some of the characteristics you expect God to have. How are your two lists similar, and how are they different? Which one do you think you might reconsider?
- What are the foundations of your life? When have they been shaken?
- What are some of the roles you play in life (such as employee, parent, provider, cook…)? How comfortable would you be, to be known as only one of those? What roles do you think God plays?

Relationship with God reveals some ugly parts

Of course, at this point we need to stop and have a bit of a reality check. For as you respond to Jesus' invitation to discipleship you are bound to discover that many who walked this path in previous generations have done so with terribly negative consequences. Indeed, a deeper relationship with God reveals some real ugly parts of the history of God's people.

A friend of mine named Tina is an accountant in downtown Toronto and someone who is in the stages of moving past rediscovering God into developing a full relationship with the Divine. Yet, she was shocked one day at the reaction of her co-workers when she told them she had become a Christian. Trusted colleagues and friends said to her, "How could you go to church? Those people are nothing but a load of hypocrites!"

Tragically, that often appears to be true. Another friend told me that when a plane he was on landed in Vancouver, the pushiest and most obnoxious passenger wore a large gold cross prominently slung on a chain around his neck. Christians throughout history have had a startling track record of persecution, crusades, wacky witch trials, and suppression of women as well as racial and sexual minorities. No wonder so many people call Christians hypocrites when all of this is done in the name of the one who commanded his followers, "You shall love your enemies and pray for those who persecute you."

Those who have rediscovered God in their lives and have wrestled with living a faithful relationship with the Almighty have also often fallen short of God's expectations. Perhaps even more importantly, they have hurt a lot of other people in the process. Building a relationship with God begins by recognizing that you are not the first to take these steps, and by learning from other people's mistakes.

As Jesus instructed his followers

Here's another old saying that deserves a second look: "Eye for eye, tooth for tooth." Is that going to get us anywhere? Here's what I propose: 'Don't hit back at all.' If someone strikes you, stand there and take it. If someone drags you into court and sues for the shirt off your back, gift-wrap your best coat and make a present of it. And if someone takes unfair advantage of you, use the occasion to practice the servant life. No more tit-for-tat stuff. Live generously. "[8]

When it came to hypocrisy, nothing pissed Jesus off more than religious hypocrites! Examples abound throughout the biographies of Jesus where he tore a strip off people who serve others not for God's glory but for their own. Jesus warned,

Be especially careful when you are trying to be good so that you don't make a performance out of it. It might be good theater, but the God who made you won't be applauding. [9]

Yet sadly we know that throughout human history many a hypocrite representing the church has done damage to others

---

[8] Matthew 5:38-41, *The Message: The Bible in Contemporary Language,* by Eugene H. Peterson (Colorado Springs: NavPress, 1993).

[9] Matthew 6:1, *The Message: The Bible in Contemporary Language,* by Eugene H. Peterson (Colorado Springs: NavPress, 1993).

– ironically, in an attempt to spread God's love. What should we say about these things? Theologian William Placher suggests this:

> *An honest response to such concerns should not try to defend the indefensible. Horrible things have been done in the name of Christ. Horrible things have also been done in the name of liberty, and peace, and Mohammed, and the workers of the world, and any number of other causes, but Christendom had a long run, and Christians have had a chance at more than their share of horror.* [10]

But how could this be? How could people after rediscovering God and now pursing a relationship with Him screw up so bad? A strong hint lies in a deceivingly simple three-letter word – sin.

[10] William C. Placher, *Narratives of a Vulnerable God: Christ, Theology and Scripture* (Louisville: Westminster/John Knox Press, 1994) pp. 109-110.

Theology of sin & the shopping cart

You may have noticed that up until now I've been hesitant to mention sin. Partly that's because there is so much pop culture baggage attached. When you hear a word like sin often you think of a creepy old priest describing dancing, a good pint of your favorite ale, or love shared between two people as "sinful." Maybe even you think back to "The Church Lady" on Saturday Night Live who searched for evil and sin underlying everything with her pet phrase, "Could it be SATAN?"

Somehow we need to rescue this little three-letter word from all that nonsense, because for as much as we'd like to live without it – we cannot outrun sin. Instead of all those other stereotypes, perhaps it would help to think of sin in a different way.

I'm sure you've shared my experience of rushing into a shopping mall or grocery store and grabbing the last cart available. Without fail (and always when you are in a hurry) you select the cart that has one screwed-up wheel on it. No matter how hard you try, you are constantly having to make corrections to where it is going. Many a day has been ruined by my struggle to overcome a shopping cart that pulls hard left or right all the way down the frozen food aisle, often causing me to take out a stroller or walker as I frantically search for the best deal on ice cream or discount lasagna!

Well, when it comes to building a relationship with God and trying to follow God's direction, often we can feel like that wacky shopping cart – never being able to follow on the "straight and narrow." Instead, we are constantly veering off left or right. We spend as much time doing "spiritual course corrections" as we do living the life that God would have us do. No wonder we often overlook the best bargains on the grocery shelves of life.

You see, that stuck wheel on our own shopping carts is what Christians know as sin. Sin is our divergence from God's way, and is a common experience for all humankind. Sin will always surround us through life and tempt us to leave God's path and veer off in any number of directions. It is part of the human condition.

For those living their lives resisting God, the word sin means very little. Indeed, they may have spun out in aisle 19 and crashed into a Kraft Dinner display and still don't even know it!

For those rediscovering God there becomes an awareness that there is something quite wrong with the shopping cart they're pushing.

And for those of us struggling to be in relationship with God, it is an on going struggle to remain focused on where we're going without crashing into someone else.

Perhaps you can relate to St. Paul's sharing of how sin affected his life:

I obviously need help! I realize that I don't have what it takes. I can will it, but I can't do it. I decide to do good, but I don't really do it; I decide not to do bad, but then I do it anyway. My decisions, such as they are, don't result in actions. Something has gone wrong deep within me and gets the better of me every time.

It happens so regularly that it's predictable. The moment I decide to do good, sin is there to trip me up. I truly delight in God's commands, but it's pretty obvious that not all of me joins in that delight. Parts of me covertly rebel, and just when

I least expect it, they take charge.

I've tried everything and nothing helps. I'm at the end of my rope. Is there no one who can do anything for me? Isn't that the real question?

The answer, thank God, is that Jesus Christ can and does. He acted to set things right in this life of contradictions where I want to serve God with all my heart and mind, but am pulled by the influence of sin to do something totally different.

With the arrival of Jesus, the Messiah, that fateful dilemma is resolved. Those who enter into Christ's being-here-for-us no longer have to live under a continuous, low-lying black cloud. A new power is in operation. The Spirit of life in Christ, like a strong wind, has magnificently cleared the air.... [11]

---

[11] Romans 7:17–8:3, *The Message: The Bible in Contemporary Language,* by Eugene H. Peterson (Colorado Springs: NavPress, 1993).

Therefore, as we grow in our relationship with God we first recognize our inherent desire to go against God's will, to return to our old ways of resisting God, but then we recognize that God in Christ Jesus is working hard through the power of Holy Spirit to keep us faithful. Our relationship with God is like any good friendship; we stick together through good times and bad.

If, in our final days on earth, we could look back on our life and our time of resisting God, rediscovering God, and our relationship with God, life would resemble a brightly colored tapestry with threads of all colors. Some threads are where we did right by God, and some are where we let God down. Although it would be tempting to snip and try to pull out those sin-filled strands where we made mistakes, the results could be disastrous. Take Captain Picard for example…

Picard's tapestry

There is a particularly fine episode of *Star Trek: The Next Generation* entitled "Tapestry" that begins with Captain Picard and a few other Starfleet officers being ambushed at a conference.

Picard sustains an injury and is "beamed up" to the Enterprise, where the lovely Dr. Beverly Crusher (who even at her age is still "not too sore on the eyes") attempts to save his life. The problem is, however, that decades earlier Picard suffered a near fatal blow to the heart by a Nausicaan alien with a sharp knife, when he got involved in a bar fight at the Starfleet Academy. This of course, was just one of countless daring, if not stupid, decisions Picard made throughout his life, and this particular incident resulted in him having an artificial heart installed which was now malfunctioning on the operating table of the lovely Dr. Crusher. At this very moment where Picard's life hangs in between life and death, "Q" enters.

If you recall, "Q" is a higher life form in the Star Trek series (almost a god-like character) who has long had an interest in Captain Picard. "Q" appears to Picard in this near-death state and offers him a deal. "Q" will allow Picard to go back in time and correct certain key mistakes he made (missed love interests, avoiding the fight with the Nausicaan so he can keep his heart and not die on the operating table, and so on) in the past.

Picard accepts this offer. After correcting his "mistakes," he is vaulted back into the present where he finds himself on the Enterprise – but no longer as the greatest captain in Starfleet, rather as a low grade science officer whose days are reduced to running little tests in a laboratory. In a profound moment Picard cries out to "Q," "I don't want this life! Put me back on the operating table! *I would rather die the man I was, than live as the man I now see.*"

To which "Q" agrees. In the end, of course, the lovely Dr. Crusher does save his life and Picard lives to serve another day.

In the wrap-up, however, Picard admits to his first officer Will Riker that when he went back in time and tried to "fix" all his mistakes, he was tugging at the threads of his past and in the end began to unravel the tapestry of his life.

Many of us can relate to Picard's story. It is tempting to pick at unsightly threads in our own background and experience. As we move from rediscovering God to a relationship with God, we cannot be frozen by the fear that we might join a long and dubious list of Christians who made some awful mistakes. Be assured, you will make mistakes. And some of them will indeed be awful. But our God is a forgiving God and the unsightly threads of our sins may be the most beneficial of all those in the tapestries of our life. After all, as long as they are visible, those threads can help us steer our shopping cart faith more faithfully down God's aisle.

Questions for reflection

- As you look back on the course of your life, where do you think your shopping cart went astray?
- What might you have done differently, if you had the chance? And how would you be different today, if you could make those changes? Were your mistakes part of your growing process?
- When you look around the world today, what are some major mistakes that you see being made? Are any of them being done in the name of God or of Christianity? How would you reason with those people or nations, to help them see God differently?

The invitation of participation in community

One last and very important aspect of building a relationship with God, in addition to getting to know God better and being aware of possible pitfalls on the way, is knowing that we are not alone. John Wesley once said, "There is no such thing as a solitary Christian." And in this, I think he was right. I have focused a great deal on moving from rediscovering God to enriching a relationship with God and this all sounds rather solitary. Of course, your own personal relationship with God is important. But it also needs to be rooted in a wider context and shared with others.

The church as God's embassy

Recently I have come to think of Christian communities, most commonly called churches, as God's embassies in the world. I was reminded of this one cool January morning when my wife Laura and I wandered the streets of Paris.

After sipping far too many fancy French coffees at a local café we found ourselves in the middle of a residential area when my bladder informed me (in French of course) that it was "Après moi le déluge." Being cheap, I refused to pay for one of those multi-franc "public toilets." Instead I scanned the horizon for help. Sure enough, just when my teeth were beginning to float, I spotted a Canadian flag in the distance. As we approached we realized it was the Canadian Embassy. From the stunning yet foreign streets of Paris I entered into a surreal world of familiar surroundings with pictures of the Queen and Prime Minister on the wall, a huge map of Canada, and people who shared my accent and look. My bladder and I knew that we belonged here.

If, by now, you're willing to risk a church again, I hope you will find most churches to be fashioned along the lines of God's embassy. You enter in from a world with a very different way of being, thinking, and acting, and you discover a group of people who share a great deal in common with you. These people are warm and inviting, a place to go when you are in trouble and a place just to hang out when times are good.

This imagery of a church as God's foreign embassy is not outlandish when you read St. Paul's letters to early churches throughout the Mediterranean. He says,

So we are ambassadors for Christ, since God is making his appeal through us. [12]

Churches, therefore, are God's embassies at work in the world, and Christians are God's ambassadors helping people who come in with various problems or questions, as well as inviting them to become ambassadors themselves. As St. Paul goes on to say,

We're Christ's representatives. God uses us to persuade men and women to drop their differences and enter into God's

[12] 2 Corinthians 5:20, *New Revised Standard Version* (Nashville: Nelson, by permission of the National Council of the Churches of Christ in the U.S.A., 1989).

work of making right between them. We're speaking for Christ himself now: Become friends with God; he's already a friend with you. [13]

As embassies of God, all are welcome. Just as anyone could have entered that Canadian Embassy in Paris – whether they were looking to use the bathroom, seeking information on how to become Canadian, or a Canadian themselves needing help with a lost passport – so too all are welcome at God's embassy. Those who are resisting God, people who have just rediscovered God, and folks who are nurturing their relationship with God are all equally welcome.

[13] 2 Corinthians 5:20-21, *The Message: The Bible in Contemporary Language,* by Eugene H. Peterson (Colorado Springs: NavPress, 1993).

Work & worship –
two main functions of God's embassy

Just as a Canadian Embassy overseas only conveys a limited picture of what Canada is actually like in its great vastness, diversity, and beauty – so too do churches as God's embassies only show a glimpse of what Christians know as the Kingdom of God. The scriptures tell us that God has a dream that one day the world will be a place free from fear and hunger, oppression, and war. This Kingdom will be known as God's reign of peace and justice where

> *They shall beat their swords into plowshares, and*
> *their spears into pruning hooks;*
> *Nation shall not lift up sword against nation,*
> *neither shall they learn war anymore.* [14]

[14] Isaiah 2:4, *New Revised Standard Version* (Nashville: Nelson, by permission of the National Council of the Churches of Christ in the U.S.A., 1989).

All Christians are called to work together to help build the Kingdom of God in the very fabric of society. Therefore, each church community gathers first to worship God and seek God's direction. But effective embassies of God go beyond just worship. They put into action God's call for peace and justice by working in their communities for everything from better social housing for the poor and vulnerable in society to speaking out against racism and other hatreds around them. God calls Christians to both worship and work, recognizing those who follow Jesus have entered into an ethical as well as spiritual life.

Churches combine the energy and gifts of all those in relationship with God in order to help establish the groundwork for God's vision of a world united in peace and justice. Through their work and worship these embassies of God's grace help shape people's discipleship to Jesus Christ as communities of prayer, compassion, and accountability. While you will never find a church where everyone agrees on the exact same way to approach things (churches are made up of people, after all)

God's embassies offer to the world a vision of the truth that will make all people free. Take this confession of faith, for example:

We are not alone,
we live in God's world.
We believe in God:
who has created and is creating,
who has come in Jesus,
the Word made flesh,
to reconcile and make new,
who works in us and others
by the Spirit.

We trust in God.

We are called to be the Church:
to celebrate God's presence,
to live with respect in Creation,
to love and serve others,

to seek justice and resist evil,
to proclaim Jesus, crucified and risen,
our judge and our hope.

In life, in death, in life beyond death,
God is with us.
We are not alone.
Thanks be to God. [15]

This kind of statement takes seriously the role of God's embassy to be a place of worship and work, where God's vision of peace and justice is enacted and where all God's children may find acceptance. Of course, you may be thinking that if this is the plan, and if Jesus as God's architect for the Kingdom of God gave the blueprints to the early church, why is the project not finished yet? A construction project 2000 years in the making seems more over-budget and extravagant than EuroDisney outside Paris!

[15] The United Church of Canada Statement of Faith known commonly as "A New Creed."

Let's look in this final section at how the journey between resisting God and being in relationship with God is both a two-way street and a lifelong struggle.

Relationship with God versus resisting God

As I suggested through the illustration of the shopping cart, living faithfully with God is hard to do. There will be many times that we slip and feel like we are moving back towards resisting God in our lives, when we become disillusioned by how our lives are compared to others around us.

One of my favorite stories in the biographies of Jesus reminds me that God knows both our ability to slip back to resistance and God's ability to pull us out of it. Picture the scene. God has raised Jesus from the dead and his disciples know it. But they grow impatient with waiting for Jesus to guide them in their relationship with God. So they decide to return to their old way of life as fishermen. One of Jesus biographers picks up the story from there:

Simon Peter announced, "I'm going fishing."

The rest of them replied, "We're going with you." They went out and got in the boat. They caught nothing that night. When the sun came up, Jesus was standing on the beach, but they didn't recognize him.

Jesus spoke to them: "Good morning! Did you catch anything for breakfast?"

They answered, "No."

He said, "Throw the net off the right side of the boat and see what happens."

They did what he said. All of a sudden there were so many fish in it, they weren't strong enough to pull it in.

Then the disciple Jesus loved said to Peter, "It's the Master!"

When Simon Peter realized that it was the Master, he threw on some clothes, for he was stripped for work, and dove into the sea. The other disciples came in by boat for they weren't far from land, a hundred yards or so, pulling along the net full of fish. When they got out of the boat, they saw a fire

laid, with the fish and bread cooking on it.
Jesus said, "Breakfast is ready." [16]

The ongoing hope of this story, of course, is that even when we turn from God and head back towards resisting God – even when we give up on God – God does not give up on us. Jesus seeks out his stray disciples and feeds them. Jesus nourishes them and leads them forward into an unknown future, promising never to abandon them.

And remember, I am with you always, to the end of the age. [17]

So we can thank God that even at times in our lives when we may feel like giving up on God, God never gives up on us. God remains with us guiding us over and over again on the path from

---

[16] John 21:1-10, *The Message: The Bible in Contemporary Language,* by Eugene H. Peterson (Colorado Springs: NavPress, 1993).

[17] Matthew 28:20, *New Revised Standard Version* (Nashville: Nelson, by permission of the National Council of the Churches of Christ in the U.S.A., 1989).

resistance to relationship with the Holy in our midst. We cannot help but give glory to God that Jesus' promise of being with his followers still remains true today. The awareness that Jesus Christ, crucified and risen, continues to come to those who struggle in faith is reflected in a Celtic blessing for Easter:

The Lord of the empty tomb
The conqueror of gloom
Come to you

The Lord in the garden walking
The Lord to Mary talking
Come to you

The Lord in the Upper Room
Dispelling fear and doom
Come to you

The Lord appearing on the shore
Giving us life for ever more
Come to you [18]

In the final section of this book, I want to share briefly my own experiences of resistance, rediscovery, and relationship with God in order to demonstrate how one can move from separation to reunion with God.

[18] David Adam, *The Edge of Glory: Prayers in the Celtic Tradition* (Harrisburg: Morehouse Publishing, 1985) p. 56.

Questions for reflection

- Just as Jacob wrestled with God all night, what questions would you like to engage God with if you met God face to face?
- If your relationship with God involves picking up the cards of your life to rebuild, how might you live differently than before?
- If Jesus is the signpost to God what lessons might you learn from his life? From his death? From his resurrection?
- Recall an experience when God felt particularly close. How might you understand the Holy Spirit at work here?
- What do you find most challenging about prayer? What might you learn about God and your relationship with God through reading God's story found in the Bible?

synagogue on Saturdays, the Protestant kids like myself to church school on Sundays, and our Catholic friends to Mass on Saturday night or Sunday mornings and catechism during the week. I went to church regularly, not so much because I believed in God in a deeply personal sense, but because my parents always promised to take my brother and me out for hamburgers afterwards.

Throughout my whole childhood, my father suffered badly from depression. When I was 13, however, my father crashed horribly and was admitted to hospital. He spent a year recovering. A couple of months after my 14th birthday, he appeared to be making a full recovery, which I later found out is one of the most dangerous times for people with mental illness.

What happened next is unclear and will probably always remain a mystery. My father was offered more and more day passes from the hospital, especially on the weekends. On one fine Sunday morning in June he was offered a day pass and went to my grandmother's apartment to plant some flowers on her balcony as a surprise for her when she returned home from vacation the following week.

While my father worked on the balcony, I was sitting in my pew at church, less than a block from the apartment. All at once something terrible happened. My father was spotted by onlookers falling three or four stories from my grandmother's balcony towards the concrete parking lot. He cracked his skull open on the concrete below leaving his body in a battered mess. While I sat in church, less than a block away, sweetly singing praises to God in heaven, I could hear the sirens of ambulance, fire rescue, and police vehicles racing to the scene. Of course, I had no idea they were making a valiant but futile attempt to save my dying father.

Whether it was an accident or suicide matters little, since the result was the same. In a flash, in half a heartbeat, my life was changed forever. It seemed that heaven and earth themselves had been turned upside down. Nothing would ever be the same for me again; I would never look at myself, others, the world, or God in the same light.

Above all the pain, however, was my ongoing struggle with God. In my mind, I thought that if God was like the all-powerful God of the Far Side cartoons sitting on a cloud with a big long white beard zapping people on earth, then he was certainly not worth following. In my grief and anger I thought, "What kind of messed-up deity accepts praise from a singing 14-year-old on the one hand, and takes the life of his father less than a block away at the same time?"

After my father was killed, I dropped out of church, once suspicious and now absolutely convinced that church was for losers and a crutch for old women who wanted someplace to go and gossip. For a while it appeared that I would spend the rest of my life in resistance to God being active in my life.

But then God sent an ambassador of Christ to my door. The Reverend Allan Saunders was the pastor of our local church. He was a man I always thought highly of, but I did not seek him out in the months following my father's death. Instead, he came to me. Slowly and gently over time I became more willing to talk about my feelings and my anger about all that had taken place. Always knowing Allan to be a man of great character, I soon realized he was also someone whose understanding of God was big enough to handle my anger and sense of deep loss. There was no blinding light, no flap of angel's wings, just a readily accessible ambassador of Christ down the street at God's embassy.

Rediscovering God in my life

For a while my only connection to God's embassy was through this one ambassador of Christ. In time, however, when I felt it was okay, I returned to sitting quietly in the last pew. I scrutinized every word, every prayer, every part of the sermon, listening for something that might give me an excuse to say, "Just what I thought; you're all full of crap and I'm outta here." But instead, I began to soak up the story of God's action in human history – through the people of Israel, the prophets, Jesus Christ, and the early church. It was a story of struggle, setbacks, pain and suffering, but ultimately hope.

My rediscovery of God came not in a blinding flash of light like St. Paul but more like the slow grinding of John Wesley, through a long struggle of sorting out what God was like and what our relationship might be. It took me a long time simmering in the slow cooker of God's love before I could even warm to the idea of a full relationship with God.

One important step along this journey came on the first Christmas Eve following my father's death. I sat quietly in the back of the church listening to the usual story of baby Jesus being born in a stable. While the story was familiar, I recognized, perhaps for the first time, how God's story at Christmas was connected to the pain of Good Friday. For even God's life in human form as Jesus was not an easy one. Rather it was a life born into poverty, and remained one full of pain and struggle until it was ended prematurely by the hands of an executioner. I had always assumed that knowing God meant one would have an easy life, but now God's experience in Jesus showed me otherwise. The easy life has never been consistent with God's blessing. That night I realized that even in the joy of the stable of Bethlehem you could catch a glimpse of the rugged cross that lay within the cradle of baby Jesus.

God's story became more real to me, as I saw that not only did God care about humankind enough to make a personal appearance in Jesus, but as a result God would be utterly despised, rejected, hurt, and abandoned in the end as Christ hung on the cross at Calvary. In the midst of Christmas joy I could actually *feel* the pain of Good Friday.

Here was a God I could relate to. Here was a God who could feel my pain. I realized that night that my old Sunday school mindset that believing in God meant you were vaccinated against all the pain in this world was never a promise that God had made to anyone – not even to his only son Jesus. The only promise that God makes to humankind is that God will be faithful in our relationship and never leave us alone. As St. Paul declared,

> *I'm absolutely convinced that nothing – nothing living or dead, angelic or demonic, today or tomorrow, high or low, thinkable or unthinkable – absolutely nothing can get between us and God's love because of the way that Jesus our Master has embraced us.* [1]

[1] Romans 8:38-39, *The Message: The Bible in Contemporary Language,* by Eugene H. Peterson (Colorado Springs: NavPress, 1993).

Through experiences like this, I became increasingly convinced that God was real and was reaching out to me yearning for a relationship. For the first time I wanted to be part of a Christian community, part of God's embassy staff, not for the sake of getting a free meal after church but because in a world turned upside down the embassy felt like home to me. God's embassy became my quiet center, as in the words of the modern hymn:

Come and find the quiet centre in the crowded life we lead,
Find the room for hope to enter, find the frame where we are
freed:

Clear the chaos and the clutter, clear our eyes that we can see
All the things that really matter, be at peace and simply be. [2]

---

[2] "Come and Find the Quiet Centre" in *Voices United* (Toronto: United Church Publishing House, 1996) #374.

Relationship with God

Perhaps not surprisingly, God and I started our relationship slowly and cautiously. The more we shared the more we learned about each other. I remembered with great fondness my own father's attempt to teach the idea of the Trinity to me. Our family farm in Northern Ireland is only a stone's throw away from Armagh where St. Patrick lived and worked. Taking a lesson from St. Patrick, my father would often teach me about the Trinity by showing me a shamrock and explaining how there is one leaf for the Father, one leaf for the Son, and one leaf for the Holy Spirit, and yet they are all one. Despite his efforts, these were things I needed to discover in my own time and my own way.

In time I did become comfortable referring to God as Father and acknowledging the uniqueness of Jesus' life, death, and resurrection as the Son of God. I also became increasingly aware as I deepened my relationship with the Divine, how God's breath – the Holy Spirit – was close to me, guiding and instructing me in faithful living. But it all took time, and I began to discover and name for myself the reality of sin in my life. I could see my own shopping cart with its stuck wheel veering off in various directions. Only by God's grace could I seem to get it back on track.

As I grew in my relationship with God I continued to discover that discipleship to Jesus does not guarantee an easy ride in life. Instead, committing one's life to following Jesus guarantees that God will always be with you, in good times and bad. As the covenant prayer of John Wesley states,

I am no longer my own but yours.
Your will, not mine, be done in all things,
wherever you may place me,
in all that I do
and in all that I may endure;
when there is work for me
and when there is none;
when I am troubled
and when I am at peace.
Your will be done
when I am valued

and when I am disregarded;
when I find fulfillment
and when it is lacking;
when I have all things,
and when I have nothing.
I willingly offer
all I have and am
to serve you,
as and where you choose.

Glorious and blessed God,
Father, Son and Holy Spirit,
you are mine and I am yours.
May it be so for ever.
Let this covenant now made on earth
be fulfilled in heaven. Amen.

In the end, my relationship with God would have been most shallow if it had not been shared with others. In looking back on my tapestry, short as it is for a Gen Xer, I can see how valuable life together with other disciples of Jesus really was for me. It is a journey that continues and it is an invitation that is open to all. As a song that I love to sing and play on guitar says,

> *The work of our God is not just for the clever*
> *The service of God is not just for the strong;*
> *The way of the cross is a journey forever,*
> *So gather to pray then we'll travel along.*

> *So welcome, welcome each other*
> *The old and the youthful, the fit and the faint*
> *Welcome sister and brother,*
> *Welcome the seeker, the sinner, the saint.* [3]

[3] "The House of Our God" by Jim Manley in *All God's Children Sing* (Kelowna: Wood Lake Books, 1992) #72. Used by permission.

So there it is, a brief sketch of my own unfinished story of resistance, rediscovery, and relationship with God.

I should make clear, however, that even though I have found this threefold pattern to be a helpful way of understanding my relationship with God I do not, by any means, intend to make it normative for everyone. Your life may resonate deeply with resisting, rediscovering, and being in relationship with God. Or it may not.

I do hope, however, that if you have a restless heart, or if you have ever felt that gentle nudge from God that there must be more to life than what you have already experienced, then this threefold framework may help make sense of your own natural movement away from and towards life with God. We are all on our own faith journeys; only you know where you stand with God. My hope for you is that through reading this book you might discover that "the truth that sets you free," that gift of getting real with God, is the Christian life not obsessed or fixated on "the right answers about God," rather it is a life dedicated to "the right relationship with God."

My sincerest prayer is that people in our own Generation X would take the opportunity to explore what a relationship with God might look like and that you might be open to the possibility that God might actually be able to change your life. After all, the God we know has been transforming people's lives for many generations now, all the way back to Jacob's day.

And while we can be sure that God will outlive Generation X, we can be just as certain that those who have a relationship with God will live in communion with God forever. In this good news we trust and say with confidence:

Glory to God,
whose power, working in us,
can do infinitely more
than we can ask or imagine.
Glory to God from generation to generation,
in the Church and in Christ Jesus,
for ever and ever. Amen. [4]

[4] A paraphrase of Ephesians 3:20-21 excerpted from *The Book of Alternative Services of the Anglican Church of Canada*, (Toronto: Anglican Book Centre, 1985) p. 214.